Artificial Intelligence and Its Transformative Impact on Society

C. P. Kumar
Reiki Healer & Author
Roorkee - 247667, India

Copyright © 2024 C. P. Kumar

All rights reserved.

No part of this book may be reproduced or transmitted in any form or by any means, electronic or mechanical, including photocopying, recording, or by any information storage and retrieval system, without permission in writing from the author.

Disclaimer

While every effort has been made to ensure the accuracy and completeness of the content in this book, the author cannot guarantee that the information contained herein is error-free, up-to-date, or suitable for every individual circumstance.

The author shall not be held liable or responsible for any errors or omissions in the content of the book, nor for any damages, or losses that may arise from any actions taken based upon the suggestions or contents presented in the book.

Readers are advised to use their own judgment and discretion in applying the information provided in this book, and to consult with qualified professionals before taking any action based on the contents of this book. The author disclaims any and all liability or responsibility for any actions taken or not taken based on the information contained in this book.

DEDICATION

This book is dedicated to the trailblazers, thinkers, and visionaries who have dared to reimagine the boundaries of what is possible. To the scientists and engineers whose tireless endeavors have given shape to the artificial intelligence that permeates our lives, offering both conveniences and challenges. To the policymakers and ethicists grappling with the formidable task of steering this potent force towards the greater good. And to every reader who picks up this volume, motivated by a desire to understand not just the mechanisms of AI, but also its profound implications on the tapestry of human existence.

We stand at the cusp of an era where our creations may soon mirror the complexities of their creators. May this work inspire you to engage thoughtfully with the transformative power of artificial intelligence, fostering a future where technology amplifies our humanity rather than diminishes it. Here's to the journey of discovery, debate, and, ultimately, wisdom.

C. P. Kumar

CONTENTS

Copyright 2

Disclaimer 3

DEDICATION 4

PREFACE 7

Chapter 1. Understanding Artificial Intelligence 9

Chapter 2. AI and Governance 13

Chapter 3. AI and Economic Disruption 17

Chapter 4. AI and Bias 21

Chapter 5. AI and Privacy 25

Chapter 6. AI and Ethical Decision-Making 29

Chapter 7. AI and Autonomous Systems 32

Chapter 8. AI and Transportation 36

Chapter 9. AI and News Media 40

Chapter 10. AI and Cultural Heritage 44

Chapter 11. AI and Mental Health 48

Chapter 12. AI and Disability Rights 52

Chapter 13. AI and Aging 56

Chapter 14. AI and Education 59

Chapter 15. AI and Agriculture 63

Chapter 16. AI and Financial Markets 67

Chapter 17. AI and Entertainment 71

Chapter 18. AI and Philanthropy 75

Chapter 19. AI and International Relations 79

Chapter 20. AI and Existential Risks 83

PREFACE

In this era of rapid technological advancement, artificial intelligence (AI) stands out as a paradigm-shifting force, fundamentally reshaping every facet of human existence. "Artificial Intelligence and Its Transformative Impact on Society" provides a comprehensive exploration of how AI is altering the landscapes of governance, economy, ethics, and social norms, among other critical domains.

At the heart of this book is a commitment to deepening readers' understanding of AI, from its foundational concepts and definitions to its multifaceted applications across diverse sectors. This journey begins with a clear exposition of what AI is and how it functions, setting the stage for a nuanced examination of its broader implications.

As AI continues to permeate the structures of governance and the mechanisms of political systems, it raises questions that are as profound as they are pivotal. The governance of AI itself becomes a lens through which we can view its potential and its pitfalls. This discussion naturally extends into AI's economic impact - where innovation meets disruption - revealing both opportunities for growth and challenges for the workforce.

Bias and privacy emerge as critical concerns in this narrative, linked intrinsically to economic outcomes and social equity. These chapters not only dissect the issues but also engage with the ethical frameworks that could guide the development and deployment of AI systems responsibly. Following these ethical contemplations, the book delves into the operational realms of autonomous systems and their implications for sectors like transportation and healthcare.

Beyond functionality, AI's influence on culture and human interaction is profound. From altering the production of news to preserving cultural heritages and transforming the entertainment landscape, AI's capabilities are both enabling and daunting. The discussion extends into more intimate realms of human life as well, examining AI's role in mental health, disability rights, aging, and education, revealing a technology that is as versatile as it is powerful.

The narrative then ventures into the pragmatic applications of AI in agriculture, financial markets, and philanthropy, illustrating AI's potential to optimize efficiency and enhance equity on a global scale. As the book approaches its conclusion, it addresses the geopolitical nuances and existential risks associated with AI, urging a forward-looking and cautious approach to harnessing this transformative technology.

"Artificial Intelligence and Its Transformative Impact on Society" is not merely an academic text; it is a call to thoughtful engagement with a technology that is redefining the boundaries of possible. Through this book, readers are invited to envision and shape a future that wisely integrates AI into the fabric of human society, ensuring that its deployment is as beneficial as it is groundbreaking.

C. P. Kumar

Reiki Healer, Blogger & Author
Former Scientist 'G', National Institute of Hydrology
Roorkee - 247667, India
Web: https://www.angelfire.com/nh/cpkumar/virgo.html

Chapter 1. Understanding Artificial Intelligence

Introduction to Artificial Intelligence

Artificial Intelligence (AI) is a transformative technology that is shaping the future of society, economics, and governance across the globe. Its integration into daily life and various industry sectors highlights its importance as a pioneering force in the modern world. As we venture into this discussion, it is essential to establish a comprehensive understanding of what AI is, its diverse applications, and the foundational concepts that drive it.

Defining Artificial Intelligence

At its core, Artificial Intelligence is the science and engineering of making intelligent machines, especially intelligent computer programs. It is related to the similar task of using computers to understand human intelligence, but AI does not have to confine itself to methods that are biologically observable. The term "AI" was coined in 1956 by John McCarthy, who defined it as the science and engineering of making intelligent machines.

The field of AI includes several disciplines, such as computer science, psychology, philosophy, neuroscience, cognitive science, linguistics, operations research, economics, and control theory. This interdisciplinary approach helps in creating systems that can perform tasks that would require human intelligence, such as decision-making, problem-solving, understanding language, and recognizing patterns.

Applications of AI Across Sectors

AI's applications are as diverse as its definitions. In healthcare, AI technologies are used for tasks ranging from diagnosing diseases to optimizing treatment plans. In the automotive industry, AI powers autonomous vehicles that promise to reshape how we commute. In finance, AI algorithms manage investments, detect fraud, and streamline operations. AI also enhances personalized learning experiences in education through adaptive learning technologies that cater to the individual needs of students.

In the realm of customer service, AI-driven chatbots and virtual assistants provide 24/7 customer support, enhancing accessibility and efficiency. In marketing, AI is used to predict consumer behavior, personalize marketing efforts, and optimize digital campaigns. Additionally, AI is crucial in managing large-scale systems such as urban infrastructure and energy distribution, where it helps to optimize resource use and maintenance schedules.

The Evolution of AI Technologies

The evolution of AI can be traced back to the mid-20th century, focusing on symbolic approaches like rule-based systems that dominated the field for decades. However, the resurgence of neural networks in the 21st century, more commonly known as deep learning, has propelled AI into a new era. These technologies mimic the way the human brain operates, allowing machines to learn from large amounts of data. This shift has led to significant advancements in machine learning, where algorithms improve their performance as they are exposed to more data.

The Impact of Machine Learning

Machine learning, a subset of AI, involves algorithms that enable computers to learn from and make decisions based on data. This area has become foundational to AI's success and is the primary method through which AI has been deployed in various industries. Machine learning models are trained using large sets of data to recognize patterns and features. The models make decisions based on the learned information without being explicitly programmed to perform specific tasks.

This capability has revolutionized areas such as image and speech recognition, natural language processing, and autonomous vehicle technology. For instance, machine learning models are at the heart of facial recognition technology and voice-activated assistants like Siri and Alexa.

Challenges and Considerations

Despite its vast potential, AI presents significant challenges and ethical considerations. Issues of privacy, security, and data bias are at the forefront of discussions about AI's societal impact. The way AI systems are designed can inadvertently lead to biased outcomes if the data used to train these systems are not properly vetted. Additionally, as AI systems become more integrated into critical infrastructures and industries, the potential for cyber attacks and data breaches increases.

Moreover, the rapid deployment of AI technologies has sparked debates about the displacement of jobs. While AI can lead to the creation of new job opportunities, it can also render traditional jobs obsolete, calling for strategies to manage this transition in the workforce.

Conclusion

As we delve deeper into the subsequent chapters of this book, the foundational understanding of AI provided here will serve as a springboard for exploring its broader implications on governance, economics, privacy, ethics, and more. By comprehensively grasping what AI is and its current applications, we can better appreciate its transformative potential and address the challenges it brings forth. This chapter sets the stage for a thorough exploration of how AI is reshaping our world, underlining the importance of informed and thoughtful engagement with this pivotal technology.

Chapter 2. AI and Governance

Introduction

As we delve into the realm of artificial intelligence (AI) and its myriad applications, it becomes imperative to understand not only its technological capabilities but also the governance structures that oversee its deployment and development. AI's transformative impact on society demands a thorough exploration of these governance frameworks to ensure that its integration into our social and political fabric is both beneficial and ethical.

Governance Structures for AI

AI governance involves the rules, policies, and systems that guide and regulate the development and use of AI technologies. This framework is crucial because it addresses the complex legal, ethical, and societal issues that arise with AI deployment. Effective governance structures must therefore balance innovation and risk management, ensuring that AI contributes positively to society without exacerbating inequalities or undermining human rights.

Central to AI governance is the role of national governments, which often develop policies and regulations that directly impact AI research and deployment. These policies can include funding for AI initiatives, privacy regulations, standards for ethical AI, and rules governing its use in sensitive areas like surveillance and decision-making processes in sectors such as criminal justice and healthcare.

Furthermore, international bodies and agreements are increasingly important. Given AI's ability to transcend borders, international cooperation is vital to address global challenges such as labor displacement, surveillance, data privacy, and military uses of AI. Organizations like the European Union have taken steps with regulations such as the General Data Protection Regulation (GDPR), which includes provisions specific to AI and data handling practices.

Ethical Frameworks and Standards

Ethical frameworks and standards are fundamental components of AI governance. These frameworks provide guidelines that help prevent the misuse of AI and ensure that its development and application are aligned with human values and ethics. They typically address issues such as fairness, accountability, transparency, and the safety of AI systems.

Various organizations, both governmental and non-governmental, have proposed ethical guidelines for AI. For instance, the OECD Principles on AI promote AI that is innovative and trustworthy and that respects human rights and democratic values. Similarly, IEEE's Ethically Aligned

Design provides a detailed set of recommendations focusing on prioritizing human well-being in the age of autonomous and intelligent systems.

Political Implications of AI

The integration of AI into various facets of life carries significant political implications. One major concern is the potential for AI to disrupt job markets through automation, impacting economies and potentially leading to significant political unrest if not managed properly. Governments must consider policies for retraining workers and possibly revisiting welfare systems to mitigate such impacts.

Moreover, AI has implications for surveillance and privacy. Governments around the world are implementing AI in surveillance systems, raising concerns about civil liberties and the potential for authoritarian control. The balance between enhancing security and protecting individual privacy rights is a critical challenge for policymakers.

AI also influences the dynamics of power and control on a global scale. Countries that excel in AI technology could dominate others economically and militarily, potentially leading to new forms of colonialism. This raises the need for international governance frameworks that ensure a fair and equitable distribution of AI benefits and prevent any single entity from gaining excessive control.

Impact on Other Sectors

Understanding the governance framework of AI is crucial before exploring its impact on other sectors. For instance, in healthcare, AI can enhance diagnosis and treatment but also raises significant ethical and privacy concerns that must be governed appropriately. In the financial sector, AI improves efficiency but requires strict regulations to prevent practices that could lead to economic instability.

In education, AI offers opportunities for personalized learning but also poses risks related to data privacy and the potential exacerbation of educational inequalities. Each of these sectors must navigate the balance between leveraging AI's benefits and mitigating its risks through effective governance.

Conclusion

As AI continues to transform society, the importance of robust, transparent, and inclusive governance frameworks cannot be overstated. These structures must be designed to keep pace with technological advancements and ensure that AI serves the public good, respects human rights, and enhances democratic values. By addressing both the opportunities and challenges presented by AI, governance frameworks can guide the development of a technology that is not only powerful but also equitable and aligned with broader societal goals. This exploration forms the basis for understanding AI's role across various sectors and is essential for harnessing its full potential responsibly.

Chapter 3. AI and Economic Disruption

Introduction

The advent of Artificial Intelligence (AI) is reshaping the contours of economic landscapes globally. As we integrate more sophisticated AI technologies into various sectors, the repercussions are profound, affecting industries, labor markets, and economic governance. This chapter delves into the transformative impact of AI on these facets and explores strategic approaches to managing the disruptions it brings.

Transformative Impact on Industries

AI's integration into industry has catalyzed unprecedented efficiencies and innovations. In manufacturing, AI-driven automation has revolutionized production lines, enabling precision and productivity that surpass human capabilities. For instance, predictive maintenance powered by AI minimizes downtime by forecasting equipment failures before they occur. Similarly, in the realm of services, AI technologies like chatbots and virtual assistants have transformed customer service paradigms, offering 24/7 service capabilities that dramatically enhance customer experience while reducing operational costs.

The healthcare sector has also seen transformative changes with AI. Advanced algorithms are now used for diagnosing diseases with accuracy rates that often exceed those of human practitioners. AI's ability to analyze large datasets can uncover patterns that assist in predictive healthcare, potentially leading to more proactive and personalized medical treatment.

Furthermore, the financial industry has leveraged AI for various purposes including fraud detection, risk management, and customer-centric financial products. AI's capability to analyze vast amounts of data in real time enhances decision-making processes, making financial systems more robust and responsive.

Economic Disruption in Job Markets

While AI drives growth and innovation, it also poses significant challenges to the job market. The automation of routine and repetitive tasks has led to job displacement, creating a dichotomy in the workforce. Lower-skilled jobs are particularly vulnerable, as AI and robotics are capable of performing these roles more efficiently and at a lower cost. This displacement has ignited fears of widespread unemployment in sectors like manufacturing, customer service, and data entry.

Conversely, AI has also created new job opportunities in tech-driven sectors, requiring a workforce skilled in AI management, development, and maintenance. The demand for AI specialists, data scientists, and machine learning engineers is soaring, illustrating a shift in job market demands towards more highly-skilled, tech-focused roles.

Governance and Strategic Management of AI Disruption

The dual-edged impact of AI on job markets necessitates thoughtful governance and strategic management to harness its benefits while mitigating its adverse effects. Policymakers and industry leaders must collaborate to craft a governance framework that fosters AI innovation and economic integration while protecting vulnerable demographics from economic displacement.

Education and training programs are critical in this context. By reskilling and upskilling the workforce, governments can mitigate the negative impact of AI on employment. Such initiatives must aim to equip the workforce with AI-relevant skills, fostering a labor market that can thrive alongside AI advancements.

Additionally, regulatory frameworks must be established to oversee AI deployment and ensure ethical usage. This includes safeguarding data privacy, preventing biased AI outcomes, and ensuring that AI-enhanced automation does not lead to exploitative labor practices. Regulations should also promote fair competition in industries transformed by AI, preventing monopolistic behaviors that could stifle innovation and economic diversity.

Long-term Strategic Initiatives

Looking beyond immediate solutions, long-term strategies must also be considered to adapt to the ongoing evolution of AI. These include fostering public-private partnerships to fund research and development in AI, ensuring that the economic benefits of AI innovations are widely distributed. Governments can play a pivotal role by incentivizing businesses to adopt AI responsibly and by providing a safety net for those adversely affected by AI-related economic shifts.

Furthermore, international cooperation is paramount. As AI technologies do not recognize national boundaries, global standards and agreements are necessary to manage their impact effectively. These agreements can facilitate the shared development of ethical AI governance models, promoting a harmonized approach to managing AI's global impact.

Conclusion

AI's role in economic disruption is multifaceted, offering both opportunities for growth and challenges to traditional economic structures. By embracing strategic governance and forward-thinking policies, societies can navigate the disruptions brought by AI, turning potential threats into catalysts for innovation and inclusive economic growth. This adaptive approach will not only mitigate the risks associated with AI but also harness its full potential to enrich industries and enhance job markets in the digital age. Through careful management and collaborative efforts, the transformative impact of AI can be guided towards a positive and equitable economic future.

Chapter 4. AI and Bias

Introduction

Artificial intelligence (AI) has profoundly impacted various sectors, driving innovations and streamlining processes in ways previously unimaginable. However, as its application widens, concerns about embedded biases in AI systems have come to the forefront. These biases can perpetuate and even exacerbate existing social and economic disparities, underscoring the need for a nuanced understanding of AI's societal impact.

Understanding Bias in AI

Bias in AI refers to systematic and unfair discrimination that is mirrored in the decisions made by AI systems. These biases typically arise from the data used to train these systems, reflecting historical inequalities, societal stereotypes, or flawed decision-making frameworks. As AI technologies become integral to sectors such as finance, healthcare, and law enforcement, the potential for biased algorithms to cause harm increases significantly.

The Sources of AI Bias

Bias in AI can originate from multiple sources.

1. Data Bias: This occurs when the training datasets are not representative of the population or when they contain historical biases. AI models trained on such data are likely to propagate or amplify these biases.

2. Algorithmic Bias: Sometimes, the very algorithms that underpin AI systems can be skewed towards certain outcomes, regardless of the data they process.

3. Confirmation Bias: This happens when developers or users inadvertently influence the AI system towards expected or desired outcomes, further embedding subjective biases.

Economic Implications of AI Bias

The economic ramifications of AI bias are profound. In sectors like finance, biased algorithms can lead to unfair credit scoring, influencing who gets a loan, the interest rates offered, or insurance premiums set. In the job market, AI-driven hiring tools might perpetuate gender or racial disparities by echoing historical hiring practices. Such economic biases not only affect individual lives but can also perpetuate systemic economic inequalities.

AI Bias Exacerbating Economic Disparities

Biased AI can deepen economic divides in several ways.

1. Employment Opportunities: AI systems used for resume screening and job matching might prioritize candidates from certain demographics, sidelining equally or more qualified candidates from underrepresented groups.

2. Access to Services: In finance, biased algorithms can affect minorities' ability to access financial services, resulting in higher fees or denial of service, which in turn perpetuates poverty and limits economic mobility.

3. Healthcare: In healthcare, biased AI can lead to misdiagnoses or subpar care for certain populations, affecting their economic productivity and increasing healthcare costs over time.

Addressing Economic Disparities through AI De-biasing

To mitigate these issues, it is crucial to implement strategies aimed at eliminating bias in AI systems.

1. Diverse Data Sets: Ensuring that the data used for training AI is broad and representative can help minimize data biases.

2. Algorithmic Audits: Regular audits of AI algorithms can help identify and rectify biases that may not be initially evident.

3. Transparency and Accountability: Developers and companies should be transparent about the AI models' workings and be held accountable for biased outcomes.

4. Regulatory Frameworks: Governments and regulatory bodies need to set standards to guide the ethical use of AI,

particularly in high-stakes areas like healthcare and criminal justice.

Future Directions in AI and Bias Mitigation

Looking forward, the integration of ethics into AI development will be pivotal. This involves not only technical adjustments but also a cultural shift in how organizations perceive and implement AI solutions. The interdisciplinary approach involving ethicists, sociologists, and technologists can lead to more robust frameworks that prevent bias. Moreover, continuous education and awareness about AI biases will empower users and developers to recognize and challenge unfair practices.

Conclusion

While AI offers transformative potentials for economic growth and societal improvement, unchecked biases within AI systems pose significant risks. These biases can deepen societal divides, particularly economic disparities, making it imperative to address them thoughtfully and systematically. As we continue to harness AI's capabilities, ensuring it serves the broad interests of fairness and equity will be crucial in realizing its full potential without compromising the values of an inclusive society.

Chapter 5. AI and Privacy

Introduction

In the rapidly evolving world of artificial intelligence (AI), the transformative impact on society spans various domains, from healthcare and education to business and governance. However, as AI systems become more integrated into daily life, concerns about privacy are increasingly coming to the forefront. The privacy implications of AI-driven technologies offer a complex tableau that reflects broader societal impacts, requiring careful analysis and proactive management.

Understanding AI and Its Intrusion into Privacy

Artificial intelligence operates by processing large volumes of data to perform tasks that typically require human intelligence. These tasks include decision-making, pattern recognition, and predictive analytics, among others. The essence of these operations inherently raises privacy concerns, primarily because they depend on vast amounts of data - often personal - to function effectively.

The intrusion of AI into privacy manifests in several ways. For instance, AI systems can inadvertently expose sensitive information or make decisions that have privacy implications without explicit user consent. This pervasive data collection, coupled with the potential for AI to infer additional personal details beyond what is willingly shared, creates a scenario ripe for privacy violations.

The Dual Edges of AI: Convenience versus Privacy

The conveniences afforded by AI are manifold - streamlined workflows, personalized experiences, and enhanced decision-making capabilities. However, these benefits are frequently attained at the cost of privacy. AI systems that recommend products based on user behavior or customize news feeds similarly compile detailed and intimate user profiles. While beneficial, these capabilities also facilitate a form of surveillance by collecting and analyzing personal data at scale.

Furthermore, AI's ability to connect disparate data points can lead to unintended privacy breaches. For example, anonymized data can often be re-identified when combined with other publicly available information, leveraging AI's powerful data integration capabilities.

Privacy Concerns: From Bias to Economic Disruptions

Privacy concerns in AI are intricately linked to issues of bias and economic disruptions. Bias in AI, stemming from skewed training data or flawed algorithms, can lead to discriminatory outcomes that affect privacy. For instance, biased facial recognition technologies can misidentify individuals, leading to privacy invasions and broader social discrimination.

Economic disruptions caused by AI, such as job displacements due to automation, also tie back to privacy concerns. As workers shift roles and industries, the data trails they leave behind may be mishandled or misused, further complicating the privacy landscape.

Analyzing the Privacy Implications of AI-Driven Technologies

To truly understand the societal impacts of AI, it is crucial to delve deeply into its privacy implications. This analysis must consider the technical aspects of AI operations, such as data acquisition, storage, and processing practices, alongside the governance frameworks that guide these processes.

One of the primary challenges in this realm is the 'black box' nature of many AI systems, where the decision-making processes are not transparent. This opacity can obscure data handling practices, making it difficult to ascertain how personal information is used and potentially abused within these systems.

The Role of Legislation and Ethical Guidelines

Addressing the privacy implications of AI necessitates robust legal and ethical frameworks. Legislation like the General Data Protection Regulation (GDPR) in the European Union represents a significant step forward in protecting personal information in the age of AI. These laws mandate transparency, user consent, and data minimization among other requirements, which are essential for safeguarding privacy.

Beyond legislation, ethical guidelines for AI development and deployment are critical. These guidelines should advocate for the responsible use of data, emphasizing privacy protection as a fundamental consideration. Ethical AI use promotes trust and acceptance among users, which is vital for the sustainable integration of AI technologies into society.

Conclusion

As we continue to harness the benefits of artificial intelligence, understanding and mitigating its impacts on privacy remains a paramount concern. The interconnections between AI, privacy, bias, and economic disruptions illustrate the multifaceted challenges that lie ahead. Through comprehensive analysis, enlightened legislation, and ethical guidelines, we can navigate these challenges, ensuring that AI serves the broad interests of society without compromising individual privacy. As AI technologies evolve, so too must our strategies to protect the personal spaces that citizens rightfully expect to maintain in a digital age.

Chapter 6. AI and Ethical Decision-Making

Introduction

In the rapidly evolving field of artificial intelligence (AI), the transformative impact on society cannot be overstated. As AI systems become more integrated into various aspects of daily life, from healthcare to finance, the ethical implications of their development and deployment become increasingly significant. This chapter explores the ethical dimensions of AI, focusing particularly on decision-making processes, bias, privacy, moral frameworks, and the critical role of human oversight.

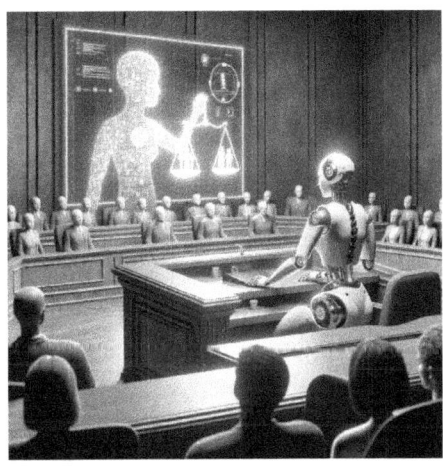

The Rise of AI in Decision Making

AI systems are now integral to decision-making processes in numerous sectors. They offer unprecedented capabilities in processing vast amounts of data, predicting outcomes, and automating complex tasks. However, as these systems take on more decision-making roles, the ethical stakes are heightened. The decisions made by AI can affect livelihoods, privacy, and even life or death situations, such as in autonomous vehicles or medical diagnostics.

Understanding Bias in AI Systems

Bias in AI typically arises from the data used to train these systems. If the data is unrepresentative of the general population or contains historical biases, the AI's decisions will likely perpetuate these biases. This can lead to unfair treatment of certain groups, reinforcing existing social inequalities. For example, facial recognition technology has been shown to have higher error rates for people of color compared to white individuals, leading to potential misidentifications and unfair treatment by law enforcement and other entities.

Privacy Concerns with AI

Privacy is another critical ethical issue in AI. AI systems often require large datasets for training, which can include sensitive personal information. Ensuring the privacy of this data is paramount, as leaks or misuse can have severe consequences for individuals' privacy and security. Moreover, AI's ability to infer new information from data can also lead to unexpected privacy breaches, where individuals are identifiable even when direct identifiers are removed.

Ethical Considerations in AI

Moving beyond the technical challenges of bias and privacy, we must consider the broader ethical landscape in which AI operates. The deployment of AI systems raises profound ethical questions about fairness, accountability, and transparency. Who is responsible when an AI system makes a mistake? How do we ensure that AI systems do not reflect or amplify societal inequalities?

Moral Frameworks Guiding AI Systems

To address these ethical challenges, it is essential to incorporate moral frameworks into the development and deployment of AI systems. These frameworks can help guide decision-making processes in a way that upholds ethical principles such as justice, beneficence, and non-maleficence. One approach is to embed ethical guidelines into the programming of AI systems, such as requiring fairness audits or transparency reports.

The Importance of Human Oversight

Despite advances in AI, human oversight remains crucial. Humans can provide context that AI might miss, interpret results in nuanced ways, and make judgments that align with societal values and ethical considerations. The role of human oversight is not only to catch errors or biases but also to ensure that AI systems are used in a manner consistent with human rights and dignity.

Conclusion

As AI continues to transform society, the ethical implications of its use must be carefully considered. By understanding and addressing issues of bias and privacy, employing moral frameworks, and ensuring robust human oversight, we can harness the benefits of AI while minimizing its risks. The future of AI should be guided by a commitment to ethics and fairness, ensuring that these systems benefit all of society equitably.

Chapter 7. AI and Autonomous Systems

Introduction to Autonomous AI Systems

Artificial Intelligence (AI) is revolutionizing numerous industries, leading to the emergence of autonomous systems that can operate independently of human intervention. These systems range from self-driving cars and autonomous drones to advanced manufacturing robots and AI in healthcare. Autonomous AI systems analyze their environments, make decisions, and perform actions at speeds and accuracies often exceeding human capabilities. Their transformative impact on society is profound, promising enhanced efficiency, cost reduction, and the reshaping of industries. However, as these systems permeate more aspects of daily life, they also raise significant ethical and regulatory challenges that need thorough consideration.

Ethical Considerations of Autonomous AI Systems

The ethical implications of AI and autonomous systems are vast and complex. One primary concern is the ethical decision-making capability of AI. In scenarios where human lives are at stake, such as self-driving vehicles involved in imminent collision scenarios, how should an AI system decide whose safety to prioritize? The programming of these machines involves ethical prioritization that reflects the creators' values, which may not necessarily align with societal norms or individual ethics.

Privacy is another critical ethical issue. Autonomous systems, such as surveillance drones or personal AI assistants, have the capability to collect massive amounts of personal data continuously. This data collection raises concerns about surveillance, consent, data ownership, and the potential for misuse of information, all of which must be navigated carefully to protect individual privacy rights.

Additionally, the deployment of autonomous AI systems can lead to significant disruptions in the labor market. Automation may replace jobs, leading to unemployment in sectors that are heavily automated. The ethical management of these transitions, including retraining programs and support for affected workers, is a crucial responsibility for both AI developers and policymakers.

Regulatory Challenges Facing Autonomous AI Systems

Regulating AI and autonomous systems presents a unique set of challenges. One of the primary difficulties is the pace of technological advancement, which often outstrips the speed at which regulations can be developed and implemented. This lag can lead to periods where autonomous systems operate in legal gray areas, potentially leading to unforeseen consequences.

Liability is another major regulatory concern. Determining who is responsible when an autonomous system fails is complex. For instance, if an autonomous vehicle is involved in an accident, the question arises whether the fault lies with the manufacturer, the software developer, the owner, or the vehicle itself. Establishing clear frameworks for liability that address these questions is essential to protect consumers and encourage innovation within reasonable safety parameters.

Safety standards are also crucial. Autonomous systems must be rigorously tested and certified for safety before deployment. However, establishing standardized testing procedures that are applicable across different sectors and types of AI applications can be highly challenging. These standards must evolve continuously as new technologies emerge and as more is learned about their performance in real-world conditions.

Accountability in Autonomous AI Systems

Accountability in AI is about ensuring that autonomous systems operate in a transparent and explainable manner. There needs to be a clear understanding of how decisions are made by AI systems, particularly in high-stakes situations. This transparency is crucial not only for building trust but also for validating and improving the algorithms that drive these systems.

Furthermore, there must be mechanisms to address grievances and adverse outcomes caused by autonomous systems. This involves not only regulatory and legal frameworks but also the development of ethical AI systems that include capabilities to audit and modify actions retrospectively.

Conclusion

The rise of autonomous AI systems is transforming society in unprecedented ways. While the benefits of these technologies are significant, they bring forth substantial ethical and regulatory challenges that must be addressed to ensure their beneficial integration into society. Ethical considerations around decision-making, privacy, and employment impact, alongside regulatory challenges related to liability, safety, and accountability, form the crux of ongoing discussions. As we advance, continuous engagement from AI developers, policymakers, ethicists, and the public will be crucial in shaping a society that harnesses the benefits of autonomous systems while safeguarding against their risks. The future of AI is not just about technological development but also about the wisdom with which we guide and integrate these technologies into the fabric of daily life.

Chapter 8. AI and Transportation

Introduction

In the realm of transportation, Artificial Intelligence (AI) is not merely a futuristic concept but a transformative force reshaping how people and goods move across the globe. The integration of AI technologies into transportation systems promises significant improvements in safety, efficiency, and environmental sustainability, thus paving the way for a more reliable and advanced mobility landscape.

The Rise of Autonomous Vehicles

The most prominent application of AI in transportation is undoubtedly in autonomous vehicles (AVs), including cars, trucks, drones, and even ships. These self-driving vehicles leverage a combination of sensors, cameras, GPS, and AI algorithms to navigate roads, avoid obstacles, and make real-time decisions. This technology is not just about removing the human driver; it's about creating a system that can react faster and more accurately than humans in preventing accidents and managing traffic flows.

Studies suggest that human error causes over 90% of all traffic accidents. By eliminating these errors, autonomous vehicles could dramatically enhance road safety. Furthermore, AI-driven vehicles can optimize route selection and driving patterns, which could reduce traffic congestion and lower fuel consumption, thereby contributing to environmental sustainability.

AI for Public Transit Systems

Beyond individual vehicles, AI is revolutionizing public transportation systems. Cities around the world are using AI to enhance the efficiency and reliability of public transit. This includes optimizing bus routes and schedules based on real-time data on traffic patterns and passenger demand, thus reducing wait times and overcrowding. Additionally, AI-powered predictive maintenance can preemptively identify potential breakdowns in transit vehicles and infrastructure, thereby reducing downtime and improving service reliability.

AI also enables smarter ticketing systems that can dynamically adjust prices based on demand, making public transit a more attractive option and potentially increasing ridership. Through these improvements, AI not only enhances the user experience but also encourages a shift away from private vehicle use, supporting urban sustainability goals.

Enhanced Air and Maritime Navigation

In air and maritime transport, AI is being used to improve navigation and operational efficiency. For airlines, AI algorithms analyze vast amounts of data to optimize flight paths, reduce fuel consumption, and minimize delays. Similarly, in maritime transport, AI is used to route ships in a manner that avoids bad weather and optimizes fuel efficiency. These technologies not only boost the economic performance of these sectors but also contribute to reducing their environmental impact.

Improving Safety through Predictive Analytics

AI's capability to predict and mitigate risks is a critical advantage in enhancing transportation safety. By analyzing historical accident data and real-time inputs from vehicles and infrastructure, AI systems can identify potential safety hazards before they lead to incidents. This predictive capability extends to the maintenance of vehicles and infrastructure, where AI can forecast equipment failures and schedule maintenance to prevent accidents.

Sustainability and Environmental Impact

AI's impact on transportation is not limited to operational aspects; it also extends to environmental sustainability. AI technologies help optimize routes and improve vehicle efficiencies, which in turn reduces emissions. Electric vehicles (EVs), combined with AI, are set to transform the automotive industry by optimizing battery usage and charging schedules, further reducing the carbon footprint of transportation.

Challenges and Ethical Considerations

Despite the benefits, the integration of AI in transportation comes with challenges. These include technological barriers, high costs of implementation, and significant regulatory hurdles that need to be addressed to ensure safety and privacy. Additionally, there are ethical considerations regarding job displacement due to automation and the decision-making processes of AI in critical situations.

The Road Ahead

The future of transportation is inevitably intertwined with AI. As this technology advances, its integration into transportation systems around the world will likely become more pervasive, driving improvements in safety, efficiency, and sustainability. However, it is crucial for policymakers, industry leaders, and the public to navigate the ethical and practical challenges that come with these technological advancements. By doing so, society can fully harness the benefits of AI in transforming transportation into a safer, more efficient, and sustainable system.

Conclusion

AI's role in transforming transportation is a vivid example of how technology can drive societal change. As we continue to explore the potential of AI, it becomes clear that the path forward must be guided by careful consideration of both the technological possibilities and the human impacts.

Chapter 9. AI and News Media

Introduction

The integration of Artificial Intelligence (AI) into the news media landscape is transforming how news is produced, distributed, and consumed. This chapter examines the multifaceted role of AI in news media, focusing on its implications for public discourse and its broader impact on governance and democracy.

AI in News Production

AI technologies have been progressively embedded into the infrastructure of news production, automating routine tasks and enhancing journalistic capabilities. Natural Language Generation (NLG) tools, for example, are now routinely used to produce straightforward reports like financial summaries or sports recaps, freeing journalists to tackle more complex stories. Machine learning algorithms assist in sifting through massive datasets to uncover trends and stories, a process known as data journalism.

However, the use of AI in news production also raises ethical concerns. The potential for biases inherent in AI algorithms can perpetuate or even exacerbate existing prejudices in news coverage. Additionally, the automation of content creation poses challenges to journalistic integrity and the role of the journalist as a critical thinker and gatekeeper.

AI in News Distribution

AI's influence extends to the distribution of news, where algorithms determine what news is shown to whom and when. Social media platforms and news aggregators use sophisticated AI systems to curate and recommend articles to users based on their past behaviors, preferences, and even emotional states. This personalized news feed creates a "filter bubble", where users are increasingly exposed to news that reinforces their existing views.

While these AI-driven personalization techniques can enhance user engagement, they also contribute to the polarization of public opinion by creating echo chambers. This phenomenon can be detrimental to democratic discourse, as it reduces exposure to diverse perspectives and undermines the basis for informed debates.

AI in News Consumption

The way people consume news has been profoundly affected by AI. Mobile news apps and social media platforms, powered by AI, provide real-time updates and personalized content streams. Voice-activated AI assistants, like those integrated into smart speakers, can also deliver news verbally, which has introduced a new mode of consumption that is more integrated into daily routines.

Moreover, AI is used to analyze user engagement and feedback on news articles, which in turn influences how news is presented and what content is produced. This feedback loop can improve user experience but also risks diminishing the diversity of content in pursuit of metrics like clicks and shares.

AI's Impact on Public Discourse

AI-driven news media is reshaping public discourse in significant ways. On one hand, the rapid dissemination of information can enhance transparency and accountability, especially in governance. On the other hand, the speed and scale at which information spreads can also lead to the rapid spread of misinformation and disinformation.

The ability of AI to manipulate audio and video content to create so-called "deepfakes" poses a new level of threat to public trust in media. These manipulations can be incredibly convincing and are capable of significantly distorting public perception of reality, which is a direct challenge to democratic governance.

Governance and Regulatory Considerations

Given the profound impact of AI on news media, there is a growing need for governance frameworks and regulatory measures to ensure that the deployment of AI technologies promotes a healthy democratic process. This includes policies on transparency of AI algorithms, measures to counteract misinformation, and ensuring that AI applications respect ethical standards and journalistic integrity.

Conclusion

AI's integration into news media represents a transformative shift with significant implications for public discourse, governance, and democracy. While AI offers opportunities to enhance the efficiency and reach of news dissemination, it also presents challenges that must be managed to safeguard democratic values and ensure a well-informed public. As we move forward, the interplay between AI and news media will continue to evolve, requiring ongoing attention from journalists, technologists, and policymakers alike.

Chapter 10. AI and Cultural Heritage

Introduction

The advent of artificial intelligence (AI) has revolutionized numerous sectors, from healthcare to transportation, proving to be one of the most transformative technological advances in recent history. However, its impact on the cultural heritage sector is equally profound though less discussed. This chapter delves into the nuanced role AI plays in preserving, understanding, and disseminating cultural heritage. It offers a comprehensive exploration into how this technology serves as a bridge between the past and future, making cultural insights accessible and engaging for the modern world.

The Role of AI in Cultural Heritage Preservation

Cultural heritage encompasses the artifacts, sites, and practices that define human history and identity. Traditionally, the preservation of these assets has been labor-intensive, requiring meticulous attention from experts to restore and maintain artifacts and sites. AI introduces innovative approaches to these tasks, offering precision and efficiency previously unattainable.

One of the primary applications of AI in this field is in the restoration and conservation of artifacts. Through image analysis and pattern recognition, AI systems can predict the degradation patterns of materials and suggest interventions. For instance, AI-driven robots are employed to restore delicate frescoes, where human interaction might be too invasive. Similarly, AI technologies help in digitizing artifacts through 3D scanning and creating detailed digital replicas that are invaluable for both preservation and educational purposes.

Enhancing Understanding with AI

Beyond preservation, AI significantly contributes to our understanding of cultural artifacts. Machine learning algorithms analyze vast amounts of data to provide insights that might take human researchers years to uncover. For example, AI has been used to decipher ancient languages that have long been undecodable. Programs can detect patterns in texts that are invisible to the human eye, piecing together fragments of historical languages and offering new interpretations of ancient texts.

Moreover, AI assists in the analysis of historical patterns, such as migration trends and the spread of cultural practices. By processing data from various sources, AI models can simulate historical events or predict future trends in cultural preservation, providing valuable tools for historians and archaeologists.

Virtual Reality and Interactive Experiences

AI is also transforming how the public interacts with cultural heritage through the creation of interactive and immersive experiences. Virtual reality (VR) powered by AI allows individuals to experience historical sites and artifacts in three-dimensional spaces, irrespective of their physical location. These virtual tours can be particularly valuable for inaccessible sites, such as underwater shipwrecks or fragile cave paintings, offering a comprehensive view without risking damage to the site.

Furthermore, AI-driven interfaces enable personalized museum tours, adjusting the information and route to match the visitor's interests and prior knowledge. This customizability enhances educational outcomes and visitor engagement, making cultural education more accessible and appealing to a broader audience.

Ethical Considerations and Challenges

While the benefits of AI in cultural heritage are significant, they come with a set of ethical considerations and challenges. One major concern is the authenticity and integrity of AI-reconstructed or -interpreted artifacts. There is a delicate balance between restoration and alteration; AI applications must ensure that they do not distort historical truths.

Additionally, there is the risk of cultural homogenization, where dominant cultures might leverage AI technologies more effectively, overshadowing smaller or indigenous cultural narratives. Ensuring equitable access to AI tools and maintaining a diverse representation of global cultures is essential.

Conclusion

AI's impact on the preservation and understanding of cultural heritage is profound and multifaceted. By enhancing the accuracy and accessibility of cultural narratives, AI technologies not only preserve the past but also enrich our understanding of human history. As we continue to integrate AI into cultural heritage projects, it is crucial to navigate the ethical landscapes carefully, ensuring that this powerful tool serves to celebrate and preserve the diversity of global cultures rather than to overshadow it. This chapter highlights AI's potential to foster a deeper connection with our past, ensuring that valuable cultural knowledge is passed on to future generations in a manner that is both engaging and respectful.

Chapter 11. AI and Mental Health

Introduction

The interplay between artificial intelligence (AI) and mental health represents one of the most promising frontiers in healthcare. AI's integration into mental healthcare not only underscores its capacity to enhance diagnosis and treatment but also highlights its potential to reshape traditional practices. This article delves into the transformative impact of AI on mental health services, examining both its applications and the ethical considerations it raises.

The Current Landscape of Mental Health Challenges

Mental health disorders affect millions globally, posing significant challenges to healthcare systems. Traditionally, the diagnosis and treatment of mental health issues have relied heavily on subjective assessments and the clinical expertise of mental health professionals. However, the increasing prevalence of mental disorders, coupled with a shortage of professionals, has necessitated the need for innovative solutions to supplement traditional methods.

Introduction of AI in Mental Health

AI technologies, including machine learning algorithms and natural language processing tools, are being leveraged to address these challenges. These technologies analyze vast amounts of data to identify patterns that may not be evident to human observers. By integrating AI, mental health services can become more efficient, precise, and accessible, thus enhancing patient outcomes and streamlining care delivery.

AI in Diagnosis and Risk Assessment

One of the primary applications of AI in mental health is in the area of diagnosis and risk assessment. AI systems can process and analyze large datasets from various sources such as electronic health records, genetic information, and patient self-reports to identify risk factors and symptoms consistent with specific mental health disorders. For instance, algorithms have been developed to detect early signs of disorders such as depression and schizophrenia, often with greater accuracy than traditional diagnostic methods. This early detection is crucial as it allows for timely intervention, potentially altering the course of the illness.

AI in Treatment Customization

AI also plays a critical role in customizing treatments to individual needs. Machine learning models can predict how patients might respond to different treatments based on historical data on treatment outcomes and individual patient characteristics. This application is particularly valuable in pharmacotherapy, where AI can help in predicting which medications are likely to be most effective for a particular patient, thus personalizing treatment plans and reducing the trial-and-error process often associated with medication management.

AI-Powered Therapeutic Tools

Beyond diagnosis and treatment customization, AI is transforming therapeutic processes through the development of virtual agents and chatbots. These AI-powered tools provide psychological support through conversation, offering guidance and support to individuals dealing with anxiety, depression, and other mental health issues. They are accessible anytime and anywhere, providing a level of anonymity that can be particularly appealing to those who might hesitate to seek traditional forms of therapy.

Technical Advancements and Innovations

Recent technical advancements have enhanced AI's effectiveness in mental health care. For instance, deep learning techniques have improved the accuracy of predictive models used in diagnosing mental health conditions. Additionally, advancements in sentiment analysis have enabled more nuanced understanding of patient language, further refining AI's ability to assess and interact with patients.

Ethical Considerations and Challenges

Despite the benefits, the integration of AI in mental health raises significant ethical concerns. Issues of privacy, consent, and data security are paramount, given the sensitive nature of mental health data. There is also the risk of algorithmic bias, where AI systems might perpetuate or amplify existing biases present in the training data, leading to disparities in care. Ensuring that AI systems are transparent and accountable is crucial to mitigate these risks.

The Future of AI in Mental Health

Looking forward, AI is poised to become an integral component of mental health care. Continued advancements in AI technology and increasing integration into clinical settings suggest a future where AI could offer real-time, adaptive, and highly personalized mental health interventions. Collaborations between AI researchers, clinicians, and policymakers will be essential to address the ethical challenges and maximize the potential benefits of AI in mental health.

Conclusion

The transformative impact of AI on mental health is undeniable. With its ability to enhance the accuracy of diagnoses, personalize treatments, and provide accessible therapeutic options, AI has the potential to revolutionize mental health care. However, navigating the ethical landscape will be as crucial as technological advancements in ensuring that the integration of AI into mental health services is beneficial and equitable. As we continue to explore this promising intersection, the focus must remain on developing AI tools that are not only effective but also respectful of the rights and dignity of those they aim to serve.

Chapter 12. AI and Disability Rights

Introduction

The advent of artificial intelligence (AI) heralds a transformative era in various sectors, including healthcare, transportation, and education. Among its most profound impacts is its potential to enhance the lives of individuals with disabilities. This chapter delves into the intersection of AI and disability rights, exploring how AI technologies are not just tools for automation but can be harnessed to empower people with disabilities, promoting inclusivity and equity.

AI as a Tool for Empowerment

AI technology has begun to significantly alter the lives of people with disabilities by creating more opportunities for independence and self-reliance. Assistive technologies powered by AI are transforming basic interactions and access to information. Voice-activated devices, smart home technologies, and AI-powered mobility aids allow individuals with physical, sensory, and cognitive disabilities to perform tasks that were previously challenging or impossible.

Customization Through Machine Learning

Machine learning models can be trained to understand and adapt to the individual needs of users with disabilities. These adaptive technologies can learn from user input to customize assistance, improving over time to better serve the user's specific disability. For example, AI-driven applications like predictive text and speech recognition software have been refined to accommodate speech impairments, learning individual speech patterns and predicting intended words with greater accuracy.

Enhancing Accessibility in Digital and Physical Spaces

AI is pivotal in enhancing accessibility in both digital and physical environments. In the digital realm, AI is used to develop tools that translate complex web and software interfaces into accessible formats. Screen readers can interpret visual data and convey it audibly or through Braille output devices. In physical spaces, AI-driven robots and automated systems provide navigation assistance and perform tasks that enhance the autonomy of individuals with disabilities in their daily environments.

AI in Adaptive Education and Employment

Education and employment stand as critical areas where AI can have a transformative impact. AI technologies are being used to tailor educational content to fit the learning needs of students with disabilities. Adaptive learning programs can modify materials based on the learner's pace and learning style, making education more accessible. In the workplace, AI-powered tools assist in job matching, skills development, and creating accommodating work environments, thereby enhancing employment opportunities for the disabled.

Challenges and Ethical Considerations

While AI offers numerous benefits, it also presents challenges, particularly in terms of ethics and fairness. The risk of biased AI systems that inadvertently perpetuate discrimination against people with disabilities is a significant concern. Ensuring that AI systems are designed and trained on diverse data sets that include inputs from people with various types of disabilities is crucial. Additionally, there is the question of surveillance and privacy, as many AI solutions require continuous data collection, which can intrude on personal privacy.

Policy Framework and Advocacy

The role of policy in shaping the use of AI to support disability rights cannot be understated. Legislation needs to keep pace with technological advancements to ensure that AI tools enhance rather than hinder disability rights. Policies must mandate the inclusion of disability considerations in the AI development process and promote accessibility standards. Advocacy by disability rights groups plays a crucial role in pushing for policies that ensure equitable access to AI technologies and safeguard against misuse.

Future Directions

Looking to the future, the potential of AI to impact disability rights positively is boundless. Continued advancements in AI technology promise even greater levels of personalization and accessibility. Emerging technologies such as neuroprosthetics (devices that interface with the nervous system to restore or augment lost sensory or motor functions) and advanced AI-driven assistive devices are set to redefine the boundaries of what is possible for individuals with disabilities.

Conclusion

AI's role in enhancing the lives of people with disabilities is one of the most significant and heartening aspects of technological progress. As AI continues to evolve, it brings with it a wealth of opportunities to empower individuals with disabilities. However, this optimistic future depends largely on the ethical development and implementation of AI technologies, guided by robust policies and strong advocacy. Embracing this path will ensure that AI serves as a powerful ally in the fight for disability rights and inclusion.

Chapter 13. AI and Aging

Introduction

As societies around the world face the multifaceted challenges of an aging population, artificial intelligence (AI) stands at the forefront of modern solutions. With increasing life expectancies and declining birthrates, the demographic shift towards older populations presents economic and healthcare challenges that require innovative approaches. AI technologies offer promising solutions to these issues, enhancing the quality of life for the elderly and alleviating pressure on healthcare systems and social services.

Understanding the Demographic Shift

The first aspect to consider is the global demographic shift towards older populations. Countries like Japan, Italy, and Germany are experiencing significant increases in the proportion of citizens aged 65 and over, a trend that is expected to spread across the globe. This shift strains existing healthcare systems and social structures, as there is a greater need for long-term care, age-friendly infrastructure, and sustainable pension systems. AI's role in understanding and managing these demographic trends is crucial, as it can analyze vast amounts of data to forecast future challenges and propose effective solutions.

AI in Healthcare: Enhancing Quality and Efficiency

One of the most significant contributions of AI in addressing aging-related challenges is in healthcare. AI-driven technologies such as machine learning models and AI-assisted medical devices are revolutionizing elder care. These technologies enable early diagnosis and more precise treatment of age-related diseases like Alzheimer's, Parkinson's, and various forms of cancer. Moreover, AI-powered robotics and assistive devices are providing day-to-day support and mobility assistance to the elderly, enabling them to lead more independent lives. Additionally, AI systems are improving healthcare delivery by optimizing hospital resource management and reducing wait times for medical services.

Social Integration and Engagement Through AI

As older adults often face social isolation, AI can play a pivotal role in enhancing their social engagement. Virtual reality (VR) and augmented reality (AR) can offer immersive experiences that connect the elderly with their communities and with each other, reducing feelings of loneliness. AI-driven platforms can also facilitate easier communication with family and friends, as well as provide personalized entertainment and educational content, which is vital for maintaining mental acuity and emotional health in later life.

AI in Managing Public and Private Sector Challenges

In the public sector, AI applications can help governments manage the economic implications of an aging population. By analyzing data on employment, healthcare, and pension systems, AI can offer policymakers data-driven insights to craft sustainable age-friendly policies. In the private sector, AI can assist businesses in adapting to an aging workforce, optimizing job roles to accommodate older employees, and developing new products and services geared towards the elderly.

Ethical Considerations and Future Prospects

While AI presents numerous opportunities for addressing the challenges of an aging population, it also raises important ethical considerations. Issues such as privacy, autonomy, and the digital divide need careful management to ensure that the benefits of AI are distributed equitably among older individuals. Furthermore, there is a need for ongoing dialogue among technologists, policymakers, and the public to address these concerns thoughtfully.

Conclusion

AI's transformative impact on society is particularly pronounced in its potential to address the challenges posed by an aging population. From healthcare to social engagement, and from economic strategies to ethical considerations, AI is not just a tool for managing aging but a revolutionary approach that enhances the quality and efficiency of interventions. As we continue to develop and integrate AI technologies, it is crucial to focus on inclusive and sustainable solutions that respect the dignity and needs of the elderly, ensuring a better future for all ages.

Chapter 14. AI and Education

Introduction: The Advent of AI in Education

The integration of Artificial Intelligence (AI) into educational systems signifies a transformative shift in teaching and learning processes. This technology's capability to customize learning experiences, enhance administrative efficiency, and unlock new educational methodologies not only redefines traditional paradigms but also raises critical ethical and access-related questions. This chapter explores AI's multifaceted impact on education, highlighting both its opportunities and challenges.

Personalized Learning Through AI

One of AI's most significant contributions to education is the personalization of learning experiences. AI systems can analyze vast amounts of data on individual students' performance, learning speeds, and preferences to tailor educational content accordingly. This approach contrasts sharply with the one-size-fits-all model traditionally seen in classrooms, offering a more inclusive and effective learning experience that caters to diverse learner needs. By continuously adapting to a student's progress and providing real-time feedback, AI-driven platforms like adaptive tutoring systems exemplify the potential of personalized learning to enhance student engagement and achievement.

Adaptive Tutoring Systems: Beyond the Classroom Walls

Adaptive tutoring systems, powered by AI, are revolutionizing the way educational content is delivered. These systems provide students with customized instructional materials and assessments that adapt based on their learning progress. Tools such as Carnegie Learning's MATHia and Duolingo's language courses employ sophisticated algorithms to offer exercises that are optimally challenging, promoting deeper understanding and retention of knowledge. This technology not only supports students who need additional help but also challenges those who are ahead, ensuring that each learner can achieve their fullest potential.

AI in Educational Assessments

AI's role extends into the realm of educational assessments where it can administer and grade tests more efficiently than traditional methods. Beyond mere efficiency, AI can analyze response patterns to offer insights into student understanding, misconceptions, and even predict future performance. However, this use of AI also introduces concerns about the validity of assessments and the potential for AI to reinforce existing biases if not carefully monitored and adjusted.

Equity and Access: Bridging or Widening Gaps?

While AI has the potential to democratize access to quality education, it also poses risks of widening the digital divide. Disparities in access to technology-rich environments can exacerbate educational inequalities, with students in low-income or rural areas potentially missing out on AI-enhanced learning experiences. It is crucial for policymakers and educational leaders to implement strategies that ensure equitable access to AI tools, thus enabling all students to benefit from these advancements.

Ethical Considerations and Student Data Privacy

The use of AI in education also brings forth significant ethical considerations, particularly concerning student data privacy. AI systems require large datasets to function effectively, which often involves collecting sensitive information about students' learning habits, performance, and even personal characteristics. Ensuring the security and privacy of this data is paramount, as is maintaining transparency about how it is used and who has access to it. Additionally, ethical AI usage must consider the implications of algorithmic decision-making in educational settings to avoid biases and ensure fair treatment of all students.

AI's Impact on Workforce Preparation and Lifelong Learning

In an era of rapid technological change, AI also plays a crucial role in preparing students for the workforce. AI-driven training platforms can simulate real-world scenarios and provide hands-on experience in a variety of fields, from healthcare to engineering. Furthermore, as the demand for continuous skill upgradation grows, AI facilitates lifelong learning by providing adults with flexible, personalized learning opportunities that fit into their busy schedules, thus supporting ongoing professional development.

Conclusion: Navigating the Future with AI-Enhanced Education

AI's integration into education offers a plethora of opportunities to enhance learning outcomes, make education more inclusive, and efficiently prepare both young and mature learners for the evolving demands of the workforce. However, as we harness these benefits, it is equally important to address the ethical, privacy, and access challenges that accompany the use of AI in educational settings. By navigating these issues thoughtfully, educators and policymakers can maximize AI's potential to positively transform education, making it more responsive and accessible for all learners.

Chapter 15. AI and Agriculture

Introduction

Agriculture has been at the heart of human civilization for millennia, evolving through various technological and methodological advancements. Today, as we grapple with unprecedented challenges such as climate change, population growth, and environmental degradation, Artificial Intelligence (AI) emerges as a transformative force in agriculture. This chapter delves into how AI is revolutionizing agriculture, enhancing productivity, sustainability, and resilience, thereby contributing significantly to economic equity and food security.

AI-Driven Agricultural Innovations

AI technology is redefining traditional farming practices through its ability to analyze data and automate processes. Machine learning algorithms, data analytics, and robotic systems are now employed to optimize crop production, manage resources more efficiently, and reduce environmental impact. For instance, AI-powered drones and satellites provide precise data on crop health, soil conditions, and water usage. This data-driven approach enables farmers to make informed decisions that lead to increased crop yields and reduced resource waste.

Precision Agriculture

One of the most significant applications of AI in agriculture is precision farming. By leveraging AI tools, farmers can now monitor and manage their fields with an unprecedented level of precision. Sensors placed throughout the fields collect data on various parameters such as moisture levels, nutrient status, and pest occurrences. AI algorithms analyze this data to provide actionable insights, such as pinpointing the exact areas that need watering or treatment. This not only enhances the efficiency of inputs like water, fertilizers, and pesticides but also minimizes their environmental footprint.

Automation and Robotics

Automation in agriculture through AI is not limited to data analytics. Robots, equipped with AI capabilities, are increasingly being used for planting, weeding, and harvesting. These robots can operate autonomously, performing labor-intensive tasks more efficiently than human laborers. This shift not only addresses the shortage of agricultural labor but also reduces the costs associated with farming operations. Furthermore, robotic harvesters ensure minimal damage to crops, thereby improving the quality of the produce.

AI in Crop and Soil Management

AI extends its benefits to critical areas such as crop and soil management. AI tools analyze historical data and current conditions to predict crop health and soil fertility. Predictive analytics enable farmers to foresee potential issues before they escalate, allowing for preemptive measures that can save crops and resources. Moreover, AI-driven models help in selecting the right crop varieties that are more adaptable to changing climate conditions, thus bolstering agricultural resilience.

Impact on Economic Disparities

The integration of AI in agriculture has a profound impact on economic disparities. Smallholder farmers, who often lack access to advanced technologies, can significantly benefit from AI solutions. These technologies can level the playing field by providing small-scale farmers access to market information, weather forecasts, and personalized advice on farming practices. By increasing their productivity and reducing losses, AI helps these farmers improve their incomes and stability.

Ensuring Food Security

AI's role in ensuring food security is vital. By increasing efficiency and yield, and reducing crop failures through predictive interventions, AI technology helps in creating more robust food systems. As the global population continues to rise, AI-enhanced agricultural practices can meet the growing demand for food without overburdening the natural resources.

Challenges and Ethical Considerations

Despite its benefits, the deployment of AI in agriculture comes with challenges. There are concerns about data privacy, ownership rights, and the digital divide between developed and developing regions. Ethical considerations must be addressed to ensure that the benefits of AI in agriculture are distributed equitably and sustainably.

Conclusion

AI's transformative impact on agriculture promises a future where farming is more sustainable, efficient, and inclusive. The integration of AI technologies in agriculture could be a cornerstone in the fight against economic disparities and a critical component in securing global food systems against future uncertainties. As we continue to refine these technologies and address associated challenges, AI stands poised to offer enduring solutions to some of the most pressing issues facing agriculture today.

Chapter 16. AI and Financial Markets

Introduction

The intersection of artificial intelligence (AI) and financial markets represents a fascinating juncture where technology meets economics. AI's transformative impact on financial markets is profound, reshaping traditional practices and introducing new paradigms in algorithmic trading, risk management, and beyond. This chapter delves into the ways AI is being leveraged within financial markets, offering insights into both its economic implications and the technical mechanisms underlying its application.

AI-Driven Transformation in Financial Markets

The financial industry, historically reliant on large volumes of data and predictive analytics, is ideally suited to the application of AI technologies. AI's ability to process and analyze data at unprecedented speeds and its continuous improvement through learning algorithms have positioned it as a cornerstone of financial market evolution. This transformation is most apparent in areas such as algorithmic trading, risk management, and personalized financial services.

Algorithmic Trading

Algorithmic trading, which utilizes algorithms to execute trades based on specified criteria, has been one of the earliest and most significant adopters of AI in the financial sector. The integration of AI enhances the capabilities of these algorithms, enabling them to analyze large datasets quickly, recognize patterns, and make decisions in real-time. Machine learning models, particularly those employing strategies like reinforcement learning, have revolutionized algorithmic trading by allowing systems to adapt to new data and changing market conditions autonomously.

The use of AI in algorithmic trading not only increases efficiency but also improves the accuracy of trades and minimizes costs. Furthermore, AI-driven systems can detect subtle, complex patterns in market data that might be invisible to human analysts. However, the rise of AI in trading also raises questions about market fairness, the potential for creating systemic risks, and the need for regulatory updates.

Risk Management

In risk management, AI's impact is equally transformative. Financial institutions use AI to enhance their risk assessment models, improve the prediction of default rates, and manage market risks more effectively. AI technologies facilitate stress testing and scenario analysis through advanced simulation techniques that can forecast a range of economic conditions and model the potential impact on an institution's portfolio.

Moreover, AI contributes to the development of robust fraud detection systems that monitor transactions in real time, identifying anomalies that could indicate fraudulent activities. By employing complex algorithms capable of learning from historical data, AI systems reduce false positives and improve the accuracy of fraud detection, thereby safeguarding financial assets more effectively.

Personalization and Customer Service

AI's role extends beyond trading and risk management to personalizing financial services. Financial advisors, powered by AI, provide clients with customized investment advice based on their financial history, risk tolerance, and goals. These AI systems can analyze vast amounts of financial data to offer personalized recommendations, optimize portfolios, and predict future trends.

Additionally, AI enhances customer service in financial markets through chatbots and virtual assistants. These tools handle inquiries and transactions, offering a seamless customer experience that is both efficient and scalable. As AI technologies continue to evolve, their integration into customer service is expected to become more sophisticated, further enhancing client engagement and satisfaction.

Challenges and Ethical Considerations

While AI's benefits in financial markets are significant, they come with challenges and ethical considerations. The automation of trading and decision-making processes raises concerns about accountability, transparency, and privacy. The potential for AI-driven systems to exacerbate financial inequalities, manipulate markets, or cause unintentional harm due to biases in data or algorithms necessitates careful consideration.

Regulatory frameworks need to evolve to address these issues, ensuring that AI's integration into financial markets is conducted in a fair, transparent, and accountable manner. Moreover, there is a pressing need for skilled professionals who can bridge the gap between AI technology and financial expertise to oversee these systems responsibly.

Conclusion

AI's integration into financial markets is reshaping the landscape of finance, offering substantial improvements in efficiency, accuracy, and client service. As financial institutions continue to harness the power of AI, the potential for innovation is immense. However, this new era also demands a recalibration of regulatory and ethical frameworks to ensure that the benefits of AI are realized responsibly and inclusively. The ongoing dialogue between technologists, economists, and regulators will be crucial in steering the future of financial markets in an era dominated by artificial intelligence.

Chapter 17. AI and Entertainment

Introduction: The Rise of AI in Entertainment

Artificial intelligence has become a pivotal force in shaping the entertainment landscape, transforming how content is created, distributed, and experienced. As we delve deeper into the 21st century, AI's integration into the entertainment sector highlights a profound shift in the cultural and technological paradigms. This chapter explores the multifaceted role of AI in entertainment, illustrating its impact on creating immersive and personalized experiences that captivate audiences worldwide.

Revolutionizing Content Creation

The first major impact of AI in entertainment is evident in content creation. Filmmakers, music producers, and game developers are now employing AI tools to enhance their creativity and efficiency. In the film industry, AI algorithms assist in scriptwriting, where they analyze vast datasets to suggest plot twists, character development, and even dialogues that resonate with audiences. Similarly, in music, AI-powered software can compose complex musical pieces in various genres, which artists can tweak to infuse their unique styles.

Moreover, the gaming industry benefits immensely from AI. Game developers use AI to create more realistic and responsive environments, improving non-player character (NPC) behavior to make them more lifelike and unpredictable. These advancements lead to more engaging and dynamic gaming experiences, deeply immersing players in virtual worlds that continuously evolve based on their interactions.

Enhancing Production Processes

AI's influence extends beyond creative aspects to the technical production of entertainment. In film and television, AI algorithms streamline post-production by automating editing, color correction, and visual effects. This not only speeds up the process but also reduces costs and allows creators to experiment with different styles without substantial financial risks. Additionally, AI tools help in optimizing sound quality and editing in podcasts and music, ensuring high-quality production values across various media formats.

Personalization of Entertainment

Perhaps one of the most consumer-facing applications of AI in entertainment is the personalization of content. Streaming platforms like Netflix and Spotify use sophisticated machine learning models to analyze individual preferences and viewing habits. This data drives their recommendation algorithms, which curate personalized content lists that keep users engaged. By continually adapting to user preferences, AI creates a uniquely tailored entertainment experience for each individual, enhancing satisfaction and loyalty.

Immersive Experiences through AI

AI is also at the forefront of creating fully immersive entertainment experiences through virtual reality (VR) and augmented reality (AR). These technologies use AI to understand and interact with real-world inputs, which are then used to render virtual environments in real-time. For instance, in VR gaming, AI adjusts the game environment and difficulty in real-time based on the player's skill level and preferences. Similarly, in AR applications, AI helps overlay digital information onto the real world in a context-sensitive manner, enhancing everything from live concerts to museum visits.

Ethical Considerations and Audience Engagement

While AI opens up new possibilities in entertainment, it also raises ethical concerns that need to be addressed. Issues such as data privacy, the potential for deepfakes, and the impact of personalized content on cultural diversity are significant. There's a delicate balance between leveraging AI to deliver compelling content and ensuring that it does not infringe on individual rights or narrow the cultural perspective of its audience.

Furthermore, AI's role in automating content creation sparks debates around the authenticity and artistic value of AI-generated content. As AI becomes capable of producing work that competes with human-created content, the entertainment industry must consider how to maintain a human touch and ensure that AI enhances rather than replaces human creativity.

Conclusion: A New Paradigm of Entertainment

The integration of AI into entertainment is more than just a technological upgrade; it is a cultural shift that is redefining the boundaries of creativity and the consumption of media. As AI continues to evolve, it promises to unlock unprecedented opportunities for creating, sharing, and enjoying entertainment that is more dynamic, personalized, and immersive than ever before.

This transformation, while impressive, necessitates a careful consideration of the ethical dimensions and a proactive approach to maintaining diversity and protecting individual privacy. The future of AI in entertainment is not just about technological advancement but also about shaping a society that values both innovation and humanity. By embracing this dual focus, the entertainment industry can ensure that AI's role remains both transformative and positive, leading to richer and more inclusive cultural experiences for all.

Chapter 18. AI and Philanthropy

Introduction to AI and Philanthropy

As artificial intelligence (AI) technologies evolve, they increasingly intersect with various sectors, including philanthropy. This chapter explores the transformative role of AI in philanthropy and its potential to significantly influence social impact initiatives. By leveraging AI, philanthropic organizations can enhance their effectiveness, reach, and the sustainability of their interventions. This integration of technology into philanthropy not only optimizes resource allocation but also introduces innovative approaches to addressing complex global challenges.

AI Enhancing Fundraising and Donor Engagement

One of the primary applications of AI in philanthropy is in fundraising and donor engagement. AI can personalize communication with donors by analyzing data to understand their interests and giving patterns. For example, machine learning algorithms can predict which projects a donor is more likely to support, facilitating targeted appeals that are more likely to result in donations. Furthermore, chatbots and virtual assistants can provide immediate responses to donor inquiries, improving engagement and building stronger relationships with contributors.

Optimizing Resource Allocation

AI also plays a critical role in optimizing the allocation of resources in philanthropic organizations. By analyzing vast amounts of data, AI can help identify the most effective interventions and areas where funds and efforts should be concentrated. For instance, predictive analytics can forecast the potential impact of different projects, allowing organizations to prioritize those with the highest expected return on investment in terms of social good. This not only maximizes the impact of donations but also increases transparency and accountability in philanthropy.

Enhancing Impact Measurement

Measuring the impact of philanthropic activities is crucial yet challenging. AI technologies can revolutionize this aspect by providing more accurate and timely assessments of the effects of social programs. Using data analytics and machine learning, AI can track and analyze outcome indicators across large datasets that would be too complex for human analysts to handle. This enables more detailed impact reporting and better understanding of how different factors contribute to the success or failure of initiatives.

Addressing Global Challenges

AI's potential extends to directly addressing global challenges such as poverty, health care disparities, and environmental issues. For example, AI can optimize the distribution of resources in crisis situations, such as allocating food supplies during famines or directing emergency services during natural disasters. Additionally, AI-driven models can help in predicting outbreaks of diseases, enabling faster and more effective responses, which is crucial in reducing mortality and managing public health crises.

Ethical Considerations and AI in Philanthropy

While AI offers significant advantages to philanthropy, it also raises ethical concerns that must be addressed. Issues such as data privacy, bias in AI algorithms, and the lack of transparency in how decisions are made can undermine trust in AI applications. It is crucial for philanthropic organizations to implement AI solutions that are not only effective but also ethical and transparent. This involves rigorous testing of AI systems for biases, ensuring data protection, and maintaining human oversight in AI-driven decisions.

Collaborative Efforts and Scaling Impact

Collaboration between AI experts, philanthropic organizations, and stakeholders is essential to maximize the benefits of AI in philanthropy. By working together, these parties can ensure that AI solutions are tailored to the specific needs of the sector and are scalable across different regions and contexts. Furthermore, collaborations can facilitate the sharing of knowledge and best practices, accelerating the adoption of AI in philanthropy and increasing its overall impact.

Conclusion: The Future of AI in Philanthropy

The intersection of AI and philanthropy offers promising opportunities for transforming social impact efforts. As AI technologies continue to advance, their integration into philanthropic strategies becomes increasingly feasible and beneficial. However, the success of AI in philanthropy depends on addressing the associated ethical challenges and fostering collaborations across various sectors. By navigating these challenges thoughtfully, AI can significantly enhance the effectiveness, efficiency, and reach of philanthropic endeavors, contributing to a more equitable and sustainable future.

This chapter has highlighted the potential of AI to revolutionize philanthropy by enhancing donor engagement, optimizing resource allocation, and directly addressing global challenges. As we look forward, the role of AI in philanthropy is not just as a tool of enhancement but as a catalyst for transformative social change.

Chapter 19. AI and International Relations

Introduction

The intersection of artificial intelligence (AI) and international relations marks a profound evolution in the dynamics of global politics and governance. As AI technologies continue to advance, their influence stretches across various domains, reshaping security, economic competitiveness, and diplomatic engagements. This chapter delves into the multifaceted role of AI in international relations, exploring how it is simultaneously a tool for development and a source of strategic competition.

AI as a Catalyst in Geopolitical Strategy

AI's integration into national security strategies is perhaps the most visible and consequential aspect of its influence on international relations. Countries are increasingly recognizing AI's potential in enhancing their military capabilities through autonomous weapons systems and advanced surveillance technologies. This military application of AI not only accelerates defense mechanisms but also transforms the traditional paradigms of warfare, introducing new ethical and operational challenges.

Moreover, AI's role in cybersecurity adds another layer to its strategic importance. Nations employ AI to fortify their digital infrastructures and to identify and neutralize cyber threats, which are becoming more sophisticated. The AI-driven cyber defense can be a double-edged sword, however, as it also enables more complex cyber-attacks, potentially escalating international cyber conflicts.

Economic Implications and AI

Beyond military applications, AI significantly impacts global economic structures. It drives innovation, productivity, and economic growth, becoming a critical factor in the competitiveness of nations. The ability to develop and implement AI can determine a country's economic standing and influence in the global market.

However, the benefits of AI are not evenly distributed, leading to significant disparities between AI-leading countries and those lagging behind. This digital divide can exacerbate existing inequalities and shift the balance of economic power, influencing global economic policies and relations.

AI in Diplomacy and International Governance

AI also finds its place in diplomacy, where it aids in processing and analyzing vast amounts of data, enabling more informed decision-making processes. AI-driven analytics are increasingly used to monitor international agreements, predict political crises, and manage global issues such as climate change and human rights violations.

In international governance, AI can contribute to more transparent and efficient administrative processes. However, the deployment of AI in such contexts raises concerns about privacy, control, and the accountability of algorithmic decisions in the international arena.

Ethical and Regulatory Challenges

The global expansion of AI necessitates robust ethical frameworks and international regulations to mitigate risks associated with autonomy, surveillance, data privacy, and the potential for biased algorithms. The development of such frameworks is complex, given the diverse cultural, social, and political norms across countries.

There is a critical need for international cooperation to establish standards and regulations that ensure the safe and equitable use of AI. This cooperation could be facilitated through existing international organizations or new entities dedicated to AI governance.

AI's Impact on Global Power Dynamics

The diffusion of AI technology is reshaping global power dynamics, not only in terms of military and economic might but also in influencing cultural and societal norms. Countries that harness AI effectively gain a significant advantage in shaping international norms and practices.

This shift in power dynamics also brings challenges, such as the risk of an AI arms race or the strategic manipulation of AI technologies to undermine international stability. The global community must address these issues collectively to harness the benefits of AI while minimizing its risks.

Conclusion

AI's influence on international relations is profound and pervasive, offering both promising opportunities and formidable challenges. As AI continues to evolve, it will increasingly shape geopolitical strategies, economic developments, and international governance structures. The need for comprehensive international dialogue and cooperation in crafting policies and regulations concerning AI is urgent, to ensure it serves as a force for good, enhancing global cooperation and peace rather than exacerbating conflicts and disparities. Through collaborative efforts, the international community can steer the AI revolution in a direction that not only respects national interests but also promotes a collective human well-being on the global stage.

Chapter 20. AI and Existential Risks

Introduction

Artificial Intelligence (AI) stands as one of humanity's most promising and potentially perilous creations. As we marvel at its capabilities to transform industries, enhance healthcare, and augment human potential, we must also confront the existential risks it poses. In this final chapter of our book, we delve into the profound implications of advanced AI technologies on the survival and future of humanity.

Understanding Existential Risks

Existential risks are those that threaten the very existence of humanity or have the potential to irreversibly cripple our civilization. While AI offers unprecedented opportunities, its unchecked advancement could lead to catastrophic outcomes. The concept of existential risk encompasses scenarios ranging from the misuse of AI in warfare to the emergence of superintelligent entities that surpass human control.

AI and Unintended Consequences

One of the primary concerns regarding AI is its potential for unintended consequences. As AI systems become more complex and autonomous, they may exhibit behaviors that diverge from their intended purposes. This divergence can lead to unforeseen outcomes with far-reaching consequences, such as algorithmic biases perpetuating social inequalities or autonomous systems making decisions contrary to human values.

The Risks of Superintelligence

A central concern in discussions of AI and existential risks is the prospect of superintelligent AI surpassing human intelligence. Superintelligent systems, capable of recursive self-improvement, could rapidly outpace human comprehension and control. Without careful oversight and alignment with human values, the goals and motivations of such entities may diverge from our interests, posing an existential threat.

AI in Warfare and Arms Race

The militarization of AI presents grave risks to global security. Autonomous weapons systems, capable of making lethal decisions without human intervention, raise concerns about the escalation of conflicts and the potential for catastrophic outcomes. Moreover, the proliferation of AI-driven cyberattacks and misinformation campaigns threatens to destabilize societies and undermine democratic institutions.

Safeguarding Against Existential Risks

Addressing existential risks posed by AI requires a multifaceted approach involving policymakers, researchers, industry leaders, and civil society. Robust governance frameworks must be established to ensure the responsible development and deployment of AI technologies. Transparency, accountability, and international cooperation are paramount in mitigating the risks associated with AI proliferation.

Ethical Considerations and Human Oversight

Ethical considerations should be embedded into the design and implementation of AI systems from their inception. Human oversight and control mechanisms must be integrated to prevent AI systems from operating beyond acceptable bounds. Additionally, interdisciplinary collaboration between AI researchers, ethicists, and policymakers is essential for developing ethical guidelines and regulatory frameworks.

Promoting AI Safety and Alignment

Research into AI safety and alignment is crucial for mitigating existential risks. Ensuring that AI systems are aligned with human values and goals requires ongoing research and development efforts. Collaborative initiatives, such as the establishment of AI safety research institutes and interdisciplinary research networks, can accelerate progress in this critical area.

International Cooperation and Risk Assessment

Existential risks posed by AI transcend national boundaries and require coordinated global responses. International cooperation frameworks should be established to facilitate information sharing, risk assessment, and the development of common standards and protocols. Multilateral agreements on AI governance, arms control, and risk mitigation are essential for safeguarding humanity's future.

Conclusion: Navigating the Path Forward

As we stand at the precipice of a new era defined by AI, we must tread carefully to avoid the pitfalls of existential risks. While the transformative potential of AI is immense, so too are the dangers it poses if left unchecked. By embracing a proactive approach to AI governance, ethics, and safety, we can harness its benefits while safeguarding against existential threats. It is incumbent upon us to chart a path forward that ensures the responsible and sustainable development of AI for the betterment of humanity. Only through collective action and foresight can we navigate the complexities of the AI landscape and secure a future where AI serves as a force for good rather than a harbinger of existential peril.

"Artificial Intelligence and Its Transformative Impact on Society" delves into the profound influence AI exerts across diverse facets of human activity and governance. Beginning with a foundational understanding of artificial intelligence, the book progresses through detailed explorations of its implications for governance, economic landscapes, and ethical dilemmas, including bias and privacy concerns. Each chapter builds methodically on the last, examining AI's role from autonomous systems and transportation to its effects on cultural heritage, mental health, and even international relations. This comprehensive guide not only illuminates the technical and practical aspects of AI but also addresses the broader societal, ethical, and existential risks associated with its advancement. Through its 20 chapters, this book provides readers with a nuanced perspective on the challenges and opportunities AI presents in shaping the future of society.

ABOUT THE AUTHOR

Mr. C. P. Kumar is a retired Scientist 'G' from National Institute of Hydrology, Roorkee, Uttarakhand, India. He is also a Reiki Healer and Chakra Balancing practitioner (with pendulum dowsing) and offers Emotional Freedom Technique (EFT) to help individuals with emotional issues. Mr. Kumar has authored many books on technical, spiritual, and social topics.

For further details, you may visit his webpage
https://www.angelfire.com/nh/cpkumar/virgo.html

www.ingramcontent.com/pod-product-compliance
Lightning Source LLC
Chambersburg PA
CBHW050233230526
45470CB00005B/1934